MARTIAL ARTS for Kids

A LOOK AT TAE KWON DO

Cara Krenn

Lerner Publications ◆ Minneapolis

For Wilson, Jack, and Nolan

Lerner Publications Company
An imprint of Lerner Publishing Group, Inc.
241 First Avenue North
Minneapolis, MN 55401 USA

For reading levels and more information, look up this title at www.lernerbooks.com.

Main body text set in Mikado.
Typeface provided by HVD.

Editor: Annie Zheng **Designer:** Mary Ross

Library of Congress Cataloging-in-Publication Data

Names: Krenn, Cara, author.
Title: A look at Tae kwon do / Cara Krenn.
Other titles: Tae kwon do
Description: Minneapolis, MN : Lerner Publications, [2025] | Series: Lerner sports rookie. Martial arts for kids | Includes bibliographical references and index. | Audience: Ages 5–8 years | Audience: Grades K–1 | Summary: "Tae kwon do is quick, exciting, and fun! From discovering what kind of kicks there are to how lessons work, readers will love learning more about this popular martial art"— Provided by publisher.
Identifiers: LCCN 2024010869 (print) | LCCN 2024010870 (ebook) | ISBN 9798765647981 (lib. bdg.) | ISBN 9798765662090 (pbk.) | ISBN 9798765656273 (epub)
Subjects: LCSH: Tae kwon do—Juvenile literature.
Classification: LCC GV1114.9 .K74 2025 (print) | LCC GV1114.9 (ebook) | DDC 613.7/148—dc23/eng/20240531

LC record available at https://lccn.loc.gov/2024010869
LC ebook record available at https://lccn.loc.gov/2024010870

Manufactured in the United States of America
1-1011023-53359-7/10/2024

Table of Contents

CHAPTER 1

What Is Tae Kwon Do?

Jump. Spin. Kick. It's time for tae kwon do!

Tae kwon do is a martial art. It is fast and exciting. Students learn lots of kicks.

FUN FACT

Tae kwon do started in Korea.

CHAPTER 2

Tae Kwon Do Basics

A tae kwon do uniform is called a dobok. It has a jacket, pants, and a belt.

Students wear safety gear when they spar. This can include a helmet, a chest protector, gloves, and a mouth guard.

Tae kwon do students use their feet a lot. They jump, spin, and kick. Some types of kicks are front kicks, side kicks, and big turning kicks.

FUN FACT

Tae means "foot" in Korean. *Kwon* means "fist." *Do* means "a way to do things."

CHAPTER 3

What to Expect

During lessons, students warm up and stretch. They might spend part of a lesson going through poomsae, or a pattern of moves.

FUN FACT

Poomsae is an event at tae kwon do competitions.

UP CLOSE!
Counting in Korean

Tae kwon do students count in Korean. They might say the numbers during stretches. Here are numbers one to ten in Korean.

One: hana
Two: dul
Three: set
Four: net
Five: daseot
Six: yeoseot
Seven: ilgob
Eight: yeodeol
Nine: ahop
Ten: yeol

CHAPTER 4

Tae Kwon Do Expert

Tae kwon do athletes can compete. They might use a mat shaped like an octagon. A match is only a few minutes.

WORLD
TAEKWONDO
GRAND PRIX
OMA 2022
make history
WORLD
TAEKWONDO
GRAND PRIX

You earn points when you kick an opponent. Aim for the chest or head. You can also punch, but not at the head.

MEX

Tae kwon do is great exercise and a lot of fun!
Are you ready to try?

Glossary

octagon: a shape that has eight sides

opponent: an athlete you compete against

spar: to practice fighting

Learn More

Corso, Phil. *Tae Kwon Do*. New York: PowerKids, 2020.
Farley, Taylor. *Little Stars Taekwondo*. New York: Crabtree, 2021.
Krenn, Cara. *A Look at Karate*. Minneapolis: Lerner Publications, 2025.

Index

Photo Acknowledgments

Image credits: South_agency/Getty Images, p. 5; Drazen_/Getty Images, p. 7; hxdbzxy/Shutterstock, p. 9; microgen/Getty Images, p. 11; Noel Hendrickson/Getty Images, p. 13; Javier Torres/Getty Images, p. 15; miodrag ignjatovic/Getty Images, p. 16; Fabio Pagani/Shutterstock, p. 19; AP Photo/Mike Egerton, p. 21; FatCamera/Getty Images, p. 23. Design elements: str33tcat/Getty Images; ulimi/Getty Images; Tuomas A. Lehtinen/Getty Images.
Cover: View Stock/Alamy.